China's Politics and Economy in 2003
Meeting the Post-Congress Challenges

East Asian Institute (EAI)
Contemporary China Series No. 34

China's Politics and Economy in 2003

Meeting the Post-Congress Challenges

John WONG
ZHENG Yongnian
LYE Liang Fook

East Asian Institute
National University of Singapore

World Scientific
New Jersey • London • Singapore • Hong Kong

SINGAPORE UNIVERSITY PRESS
NATIONAL UNIVERSITY OF SINGAPORE

Published by

World Scientific Publishing Co. Pte. Ltd.
P O Box 128, Farrer Road, Singapore 912805
USA office: Suite 1B, 1060 Main Street, River Edge, NJ 07661
UK office: 57 Shelton Street, Covent Garden, London WC2H 9HE

and

Singapore University Press Pte. Ltd.
Yusof Ishak House, National University of Singapore
10 Kent Ridge Crescent, Singapore 119260

CHINA'S POLITICS AND ECONOMY IN 2003
Meeting the Post-Congress Challenges
East Asian Institute (EAI) Contemporary China Series No. 34

Copyright © 2003 by World Scientific Publishing Co. Pte. Ltd. and
Singapore University Press Pte. Ltd.

All rights reserved. This book, or parts thereof, may not be reproduced in any form or by any means, electronic or mechanical, including photocopying, recording or any information storage and retrieval system now known or to be invented, without written permission from the Publishers.

For photocopying of material in this volume, please pay a copying fee through the Copyright Clearance Center, Inc., 222 Rosewood Drive, Danvers, MA 01923, USA. In this case permission to photocopy is not required from the publishers.

ISBN 981-238-396-4 (pbk)

Printed in Singapore.

CONTENTS

Succession Politics, Power Distribution and Legacies   1
    ZHENG Yongnian & LYE Liang Fook

China's Politics in 2002 and Prospective Changes in 2003   23
    ZHENG Yongnian & LYE Liang Fook

China's Economy in 2002 and Outlook for 2003   45
    John WONG

SUCCESSION POLITICS, POWER DISTRIBUTION AND LEGACIES

ZHENG Yongnian & LYE Liang Fook

EXECUTIVE SUMMARY

1. The 16th Congress of the Chinese Communist Party (CCP) in November 2002 marked the first ever smooth and peaceful transition of power since the Party was formed more than 80 years ago.
2. From a number of perspectives, the congress is a success. The biggest ever personnel reshuffling at the top level occurred. The practice of graceful political exit continued and the age limit is institutionalised. Technocrats remain in power, with younger and better-educated cadres recruited into the top leadership.
3. Nevertheless, the distribution of power among factions is uneven. Although Hu Jintao ranks the highest in the Politburo Standing Committee, he lacks factional support. So does Wen Jiabao, slated to be Premier in March 2003. In contrast, Jiang Zemin, despite relinquishing his senior party post, can count six supporters among the nine members of the Politburo Standing Committee. However, Jiang's faction may not be monolithic.
4. There is greater representation of provinces in the Politburo. Among the provinces, the bias is towards the coastal provinces. The Party has recognised the importance the coastal provinces have played and will continue to play in China's economic development and is thus willing to allow these provinces a greater say in the Party's highest decision-making body.
5. As for the inland provinces, their representation is more symbolic. The Party wants to show the importance it attaches to spreading wealth to the inland provinces. The inclusion of Xinjiang in the Politburo indicates the Party's determination to contain separatist movements there.

6. The *"taizidang"* or offspring of party elders have emerged as a significant political force. They are considered by the Party to be reliable and loyal. Also, a number of them have proven themselves to be capable and deserving of the posts they currently occupy.
7. The Party remains in control of the military. No military man is appointed to the Politburo Standing Committee, and in accordance with past practice, two representatives of the military are appointed to the Politburo. Jiang remains in control of the PLA as Chairman, Central Military Commission.
8. Jiang has secured for himself a place alongside Mao Zedong and Deng Xiaoping. The inclusion of the "Three Represents" theory into the Party Constitution marks the culmination of years of efforts by Jiang to widen the social base of the Party and ensure it stays relevant. The Party Constitution was also changed to reflect the Party as the vanguard not only of the working class, but also of the Chinese nation and Chinese people.
9. Equally important is Jiang's vision to transform the whole of China into a *xiaokang shehui* (comfortable society). Jiang has set the target of quadrupling China's GDP by 2020 with 2000 as base year.
10. As General Secretary, Hu Jintao has pledged that on important matters he would seek instruction from and listen to the views of his predecessor. Not surprisingly, Hu has stated that he will continue with Jiang's policies. He is unlikely to introduce any radical policies that would complicate his efforts at consolidating power.
11. In the initial years, Hu will have a tough time being his own man given the predominance of Jiang's faction and Jiang's likely continued involvement in some key decision-making areas such as military affairs and foreign relations, especially Taiwan affairs.

SUCCESSION POLITICS, POWER DISTRIBUTION AND LEGACIES

ZHENG Yongnian & LYE Liang Fook

Smooth Leadership Transition

The 16th Congress of the Chinese Communist Party (CCP), convened in Beijing from November 8–14, 2002, marked the first ever smooth and peaceful transition of power since the Party was formed more than 80 years ago. Neither Mao Zedong nor Deng Xiaoping, despite their impeccable revolutionary credentials, successfully transferred power to their chosen successors. Then appointed successors Lin Biao, Liu Shaoqi, Hu Yaobang and Zhao Zhiyang all fell by the wayside. In contrast, Jiang Zemin, a technocrat whom detractors dismissed as no more than a mere seat-warmer in 1989, has presided over such an unprecedented transition. This is all the more significant as Hu Jintao was not even Jiang's preferred successor.

Although the 16th Party Congress has ended, the outcomes of the congress continue to grip the attention of China watchers, including government leaders and officials, academics and businessmen. They remain interested in the key personnel changes, new power configuration, amendments to the Party Constitution and their implications. There is so far no dearth of preliminary comments related to the 16th Party Congress in the media. This paper summarises some of the major outcomes.

Changes in the Leadership Structure

All six of the previous seven-member Politburo Standing Committee, other than Hu Jintao, stepped down as they have reached or are beyond the mandatory retirement age limit of 70. As for Li Ruihuan, he has been forced by Jiang to retire although he is only 68. Jiang did not want Li Ruihuan to remain in the Political Bureau Standing Committee as the latter had disagreed with Jiang frequently and would have no qualms riding roughshod over Jiang's men. The "New Three Talks" enunciated by Jiang before the 16th Party Congress was Jiang's way of exerting pressure on Li Ruihuan to step down in the interest of "Solidarity, the Big Picture and Stability." In stepping down, Li Ruihuan followed the Qiao Shi's model of making a reluctant but graceful political exit.

Table 1 shows the members of the Politburo and its Standing Committee. The 16th Party Congress witnessed the continued trend of electing younger and better-educated leaders. In the expanded Politburo Standing Committee, eight of its nine members are new. Within the Politburo, fifteen out of its sixteen members (excluding its Standing Committee) are new. Only Madam Wu Yi moved up from an alternate member in the last Politburo to become a full member in the present Politburo. The average age of all Politburo members is 60.6, compared with the average age of 63 for the 15th Congress, 62 for the 14th, 64 for the13th and 72 for the 12th.

All Politburo members have at least college education and above. The trend towards a technocratic leadership has continued unabated. Like the last Politburo, the majority of the present Politburo

Table 1. The Political Bureau and its Standing Committee at the 16th Party Congress (2002)

	Name	Age	Education
Members of Standing Committee Average age: 62.1	Hu Jintao	60	Qinghua Univ.
	Wu Bangguo*	61	Qinghua Univ.
	Wen Jiabao*	60	Beijing Geology Institute
	Jia Qinglin*	62	Hebei Engrg. Institute
	Zeng Qinghong*	63	Beijing Engrg. Institute
	Huang Ju*	64	Qinghua Univ.
	Wu Guanzheng*	64	Qinghua Univ.
	Li Changchun*	58	Ha'erbin Industrial Univ.
	Luo Gan*	67	Beijing Steel Institute
Members of Political Bureau (excluding Standing Committee) Average age: 59.8	Wang Lequan*	58	Central Party School
	Wang Zhaoguo*	61	Ha'erbin Univ.
	Hui Liangyu*	58	Jilin Provincial Party School
	Liu Qi*	60	Beijing Steel Institute
	Liu Yunshan*	55	Central Party School
	Wu Yi	64	Beijing Petroleum Institute
	Zhang Lichang*	64	Beijing Economic Institute
	Zhang Dejiang*	56	(North) Korea Univ.
	Chen Liangyu*	56	PLA Military Engrg. School
	Zhou Yongkang*	60	Beijing Petroleum Institute
	Yu Zhengsheng*	55	Ha'erbin Military Engrg. Institute
	He Guoqiang*	59	Beijing Chemistry Engrg. Institute
	Guo Boxiong*	60	PLA Military School
	Cao Gangchuan*	67	Soviet Union military school
	Zeng Beiyan*	64	Qinghua Univ.
	Wang Gang* (alternate)	60	Jilin Univ.

* Newly recruited members
(See Appendix for the Political Bureau and its Standing Committee at the 15th Party Congress)

members have an engineering background. Within the Politburo Standing Committee, all members are engineers, in contrast to the last Politburo Standing Committee where Li Ruihuan and Li Lanqing were not from an engineering background. Another important difference is that unlike Jiang Zemin, Li Peng, Wei Jianxing and Li Lanqing who had studied overseas such as in the then-Soviet Union, the current crop of Politburo Standing Committee members received their education in China. In other words, they have no overseas educational experience compared to their predecessors.

Within the Politburo, there are three members with social sciences and Central Party School backgrounds. Wang Gang, an alternate Politburo member, is a graduate from the Philosophy Department of Jilin University. Wang Lequan and Liu Yunshan graduated from the Central Party School. Their appointment signifies the Party's emphasis on internal reform to stay relevant to the changing socio-economic dynamics in the country.

In the Central Committee, 180 of its 356 members or 50.6 per cent are new entrants. Such a scale of rejuvenation is large by recent standards. Table 2 shows that the average age of the Central Committee member is 55.4, compared with 56, 56, 55 and 62, respectively, in the four preceding congresses. There is also a progressively younger crop of leaders in the Politburo and its Standing Committee.

Table 2 also shows that in terms of education, the percentage of Central Committee members having college education and above is 98.6, compared with 92 for the 15th Congress, 84 for the 14th, 73 for the 13th and 55 for the 12th. It would appear from the above that promotion to the Central Committee and Politburo will increasingly be based on education and performance although who one knows will continue to be important but would not be the sole deciding criterion.

Table 2. Changes in Average Age of Members of the CCP Leadership, 1982–2002
(includes education level of Central Committee members)

Congress/Year	Members of Central Committee		Members of Political Bureau Standing Committee	Members of Political Bureau
	Age	With college and above education (%)		
12th (1982)	62	55.4	73.8	71.8
13th (1987)	55.2	73.3	63.6	64
14th (1992)	56.3	83.7	63.4	61.9
15th (1997)	55.9	92.4	65.4	62.9
16th (2002)	55.4	98.6	62.1	60.6

Distribution of Power

Although Hu Jintao ranks the highest in the Politburo Standing Committee, he lacks factional support. There is virtually no one in the Politburo Standing Committee whom he can count on for support. Wen Jiabao, slated to be the Premier in March 2003, appears much like a loner in the Politburo. In his political career, Wen has been careful to shun factional politics, a reason that has contributed to his political longevity. Known as the "humpty dumpty" in China's political circles, Wen has outlasted three of his mentors namely Hu Yaobang, Zhao Zhiyang and Jiang Zemin. Like Zhu Rongji, Wen is expected to focus his energy on tackling the serious challenges confronting the economy rather than engage in factional politicking.

In contrast, Jiang, even though he has relinquished his senior party post, can count on six supporters among the nine members of the Politburo Standing Committee. They include Wu Bangguo, Jia Qinglin, Zeng Qinghong, Huang Ju, Wu Guanzheng and Li

Changchun. Another factor in Jiang's favour is the disappearance of the Qiao Shi's faction in the Politburo Standing Committee.

At the 1997 15th Party Congress, although Jiang succeeded in forcing Qiao Shi to step down from the Politburo, he still had to contend with Qiao's supporters, Wei Jianxing and Tian Jiyun. With both stepping down, Jiang's faction has even greater room to manoeuvre. Given the influence Jiang still wields, it is not surprising that the media has portrayed Hu as a hapless leader under Jiang's shadow, with headlines such as "Hu's in Charge?",[1] "Hu pledges to confer with Jiang on issues",[2] "The Shanghai faction consolidates its grip on power",[3] and "Is Hu going to be [a] lame-duck leader?"[4]

However, Jiang's faction may not be monolithic, due mainly to factions among his own men which will make it difficult for them to work together as a unit. There are essentially two groups. The first, the Shanghai Gang, comprises Wu Bangguo (likely to be NPC Chairman), Zeng Qinghong (likely to be in-charge of party and foreign affairs) and Huang Ju (likely to be with the State Council). The second group, Jiang's loyalists, comprises Jia Qinglin (likely to be CPPCC Chairman), Li Changchun (likely to be in charge of propaganda) and Wu Guangzheng (in-charge of General Discipline Inspection Commission).

There could even be factions within the two groups. For instance, Huang Ju is reputed to be calculating and may not be able to get along with Zeng Qinghong. Also, as Jiang's men are holding key positions in different party and government organisations, they may ultimately have to be more accountable to the institutions that they represent. Furthermore, one cannot rule out the possibility of one or two of Jiang's men trying to get close to Hu to ensure their long-term

---

[1] *Time (Asia)*, November 25, 2002.
[2] *International Herald Tribune*, November 21, 2002.
[3] *South China Morning Post*, November 16, 2002.
[4] *The Sunday Times*, November 17, 2002.

political survival. Such intrigue will get more intense as Jiang gets more advanced in years.

Greater Provincial and *"Taizidang"* Representation

An interesting outcome of the 16th Party Congress is the greater representation of the provinces in the Politburo. In the Politburo Standing Committee, there is now a relative balance between representation of Beijing and that of the provinces. Table 3 shows that four out of the nine members, namely Jia Qinglin (Beijing), Huang Ju (Shanghai), Wu Guanzheng (Shangdong) and Li Changchun (Guangdong), are from the provinces and cities. Looking at the Politburo as a whole, the balance is in favour of provincial

Table 3. Growing Provincial Representation

	Name	Local Base
Standing Committee	Jia Qinglin	Beijing
	Huang Ju	Shanghai
	Wu Guanzheng	Shandong
	Li Changchun	Guangdong
Political Bureau	Wang Liquan	Xinjiang
	Hui Liangyu	Jiangsu
	Liu Qi	Beijing
	Zhang Lichang	Tianjin
	Zhang Dejiang	Zhejiang
	Chen Liangyu	(Guangdong)
	Zhou Yongkang	Shanghai
	Yu Zhengsheng	Sichuan
	He Guoqiang	Hubei
		Chongqing

representation. Thirteen out of the twenty-four Politburo members or 54.2 per cent come from the provinces. Such a heavy representation of the provinces in the highest leadership has never taken place in previous party congresses where most leaders came from central bureaucracies.

Table 4 shows that among the thirteen provincial leaders, the bias is towards the coastal provinces, namely Beijing, Shanghai, Shandong, Guangdong, Jiangsu, Tianjin and Zhejiang. This is due to the Party's recognition of the importance the coastal provinces have played and will continue to play in China's economic development and its willingness to allow these provinces a greater say in the Party's highest decision-making body. Also, the support of the coastal provinces is crucial in order to effectively carry out the western development strategy, which will be a key area of focus under Hu.

Table 4. Representation of Coastal and Inland Provinces

	Name	Province
Coastal	Jia Qinglin	Beijing
	Huang Ju	Shanghai
	Wu Guanzheng	Shandong
	Li Changchun	Guangdong
	Hui Liangyu	Jiangsu
	Liu Qi	Beijing
	Zhang Lichang	Tianjin
	Zhang Dejiang	Zhejiang (Guangdong)
	Chen Liangyu	Shanghai
Inland	Wang Lequan	Xinjiang
	Zhou Yongkang	Sichuan
	Yu Zhengsheng	Hubei
	He Guoqiang	Chongqing

There are only four inland provinces represented in the Politburo, namely Xinjiang, Sichuan, Hubei and Chongqing. Although the figure is more than the previous Politburo, the representation of inland provinces is still symbolic. One could surmise that the leadership wants to show it attaches importance to spreading wealth to the inland provinces. The inclusion of Xinjiang in the Politburo for the first time indicates the Party's commitment not only to bring economic progress and prosperity to the province but also its determination to contain separatist movements there.

Yet another significant outcome of the 16th Party Congress is the emergence of so-called "*taizidang*" or offspring of party elders. This group had been deliberately sidelined for at least the past 10 years. Deng Xiaoping had denied them access to power for fear of evoking ill-will among the people.[5] Under Deng, memories of the 1989 Tiananmen incident where students called on the Party to rid itself of political favouritism and nepotism were still vivid. At that time, being associated with a *taizidang* was more a political liability than an asset.

In contrast, the 16th Party Congress and its aftermath saw much greater prominence accorded to *taizidang* in the power hierarchy. Table 5 shows several who have risen to prominence recently. Foremost among them is Zeng Qinghong, member of the Politburo Standing Committee and son of Zeng Shan, who was former Minister of Internal Affairs. Others include Yu Zhengsheng (Party Secretary, Hubei), Xi Jinping (Party Secretary, Zhejiang), Bai Keming (Party Secretary, Hebei), Wang Qishan (Party Secretary, Hainan), Bo Xilai (Governor, Liaoning) and Hong Hu (Governor, Jilin).

The emergence of *taizidang* can be attributed to the following three reasons: First, they are considered by the Party to be reliable

---

[5] *Straits Times*, August 3, 2001.

Table 5. The Rise of *Taizidang* (Princelings)

Name	Present Position	Family Background
Zeng Qinghong	Politburo Standing Committee Member	Son of Zeng Shan, Minister of Internal Affairs
Yu Zhengsheng	Party Secretary, Hubei	Son of Huang Jin, Mayor of Tianjin
Xi Jinping	Party Secretary, Zhejiang	Son of Xi Zhongxiong, PLA General
Bai Keming	Party Secretary, Hebei	Son of Bai Jian, Deputy Minister of First Mechanical Industry
Wang Qishan	Party Secretary, Hainan	Son-in-law of Yao Yilin, Politburo Standing Committee member
Bo Xilai	Governor, Liaoning	Son of Bo Yibo, Politburo member
Hong Hu	Governor, Jilin	Son of Hong Xiuzhi, PLA general

and loyal, particularly at a time when the Party faces many daunting challenges. Second, a number of *taizidang* have proven themselves to be capable and deserving of the posts they currently occupy. In other words, meritocracy also applies to the *taizidang*. Third, unlike the Deng period, where it was politically sensitive to promote the sons of party elders who were still alive, there is less need for such caution now as many of these elders are no longer around.

Party Still Controls the Gun

The 16th Party Congress once again reaffirms that the Party remains in control of the military. In line with the tradition set at the 15th Party Congress, no military man is appointed to the Politburo

Standing Committee. Also, in accordance with previous practice, two representatives of the military, Guo Boxiong and Cao Gangchuan, are appointed to the Politburo. Table 6 shows that Guo Boxiong and Cao Gangchuan are also concurrently Vice Chairmen of the Central Military Commission (CMC).

Table 6. The Central Military Commission

	Previous Members	Present Members
Chairman	Jiang Zemin (1926)	Jiang Zemin (1926)
Vice Chairmen	Hu Jintao (1942) Zhang Wannian (1928) Chi Haotian (1929)	Hu Jintao (1942) Guo Boxiong (1942) Cao Gangchuan (1935)
CMC Members	Fu Quanyou (1930) Wang Ke (1931) Yu Yongbo (1931) Wang Ruilin (1929) Guo Boxiong (1942) Xu Caihuo (1943) Cao Gangchuan (1935)	Xu Caihuo Liang Gaunglie (1940) Liao Xilong (1940) Li Jinai (1942)

Jiang Zemin, a civilian and a non-Central Committee member, remains in control of the PLA as CMC Chairman. Jiang appears to be following in the footsteps of Deng, who was CMC Chairman from 1987 to 1989 even though he was not a Central Committee member. It is, however, unclear how long Jiang intends to hold on to this position. Some analysts have speculated that Jiang is likely to step down from his CMC post in March 2003 when he will have to relinquish his post as President. Others predict that he will stay on for a bit longer. An article in the *Asian Wall Street Journal* even suggests that Jiang could stay on for at least three years. The article quoted an aide of Jiang who revealed what Jiang told foreign dignitaries calling on him.[6]

Within the CMC, other than Jiang Zemin and Hu Jintao, six out of its nine generals have stepped down. There are three significant points about the CMC set-up. First, with the exception of Jiang Zemin (76) and Cao Gangchuan (67), the rest of the members are around 60 years of age. This places them among the fourth generation of leaders and contemporaries to Hu. Second, only three of the six vacated military spots are replaced. They are by Liang Guanglie (62, Chief, PLA General Staff), Liao Xilong (62, Director, General Logistics Department) and Li Jinai (60, Chief, General Armaments Department). The main reason for not filling up all the vacated positions is perhaps to leave room for Hu to make his own appointments in the future. Third, like the Politburo Standing Committee, some sort of factional balance has been achieved in the CMC. The two retired generals, Zhang Wannian, former Vice Chairman of CMC, and Fu Quanyou, former Chief of General Staff, have ensured that their own men assumed positions in the CMC.

Table 7 shows the background of the CMC members. Zhang Wannian's supporters in the CMC include Guo Boxiong (served under Zhang as Deputy Commander, Beijing Military Region), Li Jinai (served under Zhang when he was Commander, Jinan Military Region) and Xu Caihou (who takes over from Zhang as the key go-between for the Party and the PLA nerve centres). Fu Quanyou's supporters in the CMC include Liao Xilong who fought in the war against Vietnam in 1979 and together with Fu, helped to enforce martial law when it was declared in Lhasa in March 1989. Interestingly, that was also the time when Hu Jintao was Party Secretary of Tibet. Liao Xilong is reported to be Hu's ally.

---

[6] *The Asian Wall Street Journal*, November 28, 2002.

Table 7. Background of CMC Members of the 16th Party Congress

Name	Background
Jiang Zemin	Chairman, CMC
Hu Jintao	Vice Chairman, CMC
Guo Boxiong	Executive Deputy Chief, General Staff Headquarters; Commander, Lanzhou Military Region and Deputy Commander, Beijing Military Region
Cao Gangchuan	Director, General Armament Dept.; Deputy Commander, Vietnam War
Xu Caihou	Executive Deputy Director, General Political Dept.; Political Commissar, Jinan Military Region
Liang Guanglie	Commander, Nanjing Military Region. Also served in Jinan Military Region and Beijing Military Region
Liao Xilong	Commander, Chengdu Military Region
Li Jinai	Political Commissar, General Armament Dept.; Political Commissar, Commission of Science, Technology & Industry for National Defence

The question arises as to whether Hu can command the military as effectively as Jiang. This is crucial if Hu is to succeed in consolidating power. To some extent, Hu can hope to build on Jiang's success in institutionalising party-military relations. Some of Jiang's initiatives included creating a more professional PLA; promoting generals to key positions in the military; promulgating the National Defence Law of 1997 that established the Party's legal control over the military; de-linking the military from business; and, increasing the military's defence spending at double-digit rates every year since 1989. Other than institutional means, and perhaps more important, Hu will have to win over the trust and confidence of the PLA. This will take time.

Jiang's Legacy

Jiang has secured for himself a place alongside China's two great leaders, Mao Zedong and Deng Xiaoping. This was partly because of Jiang's success in managing the Chinese economy and elevating China's international status. China is now a WTO member and will host the 2008 Olympics. It is also a constructive player in the US war on terrorism. China is arguably the only successful and most powerful remaining communist bastion.

Closer to home, Jiang has strengthened the basis for the Party's continued monopoly on power possibly for many more years to come. The inclusion of the "Three Represents" theory into the Party Constitution marks the culmination of years of efforts by Jiang to widen the social base of the Party by admitting capitalists as well as to ensure it stays relevant. The preamble of the Party Constitution was also changed to reflect the Chinese Communist Party as the vanguard not only of the working class, but also of the Chinese nation and Chinese people. This is a significant move by the Party to distance itself from any distinct social class and move towards a political entity that will represent and coordinate the interests of various social classes. What kind of political entity the Party will ultimately evolve into remains to be seen.

Most attention in the western media has focused primarily on the "Three Represents" theory and its significance, but this does not fully explain Jiang's legacy. Equally important, if not more so, is Jiang's vision to transform the whole of China into a *xiaokang shehui* (comfortable society), which was the title of his political report to the 16th Party Congress. The goal is to lay a firm foundation for achieving full-scale modernisation by 2050. According to Jiang, China has already accomplished the first of two steps towards modernisation set by Deng twenty years ago.[7] Building on previous successes, Jiang has set the target of quadrupling China's GDP by 2020 with 2000 as base year.[8]

Hu in Jiang's Shadow

As General Secretary, Hu is careful not to appear to upstage Jiang. Apparently, in his acceptance speech after being named General Secretary, Hu pledged that on important matters he would seek instruction from and listen to the views of his predecessor.[9] Even publicly, Hu has deliberately refrained from a high profile since becoming General Secretary. At official functions, Jiang's name continues to appear before Hu's. The Party's mouthpiece, the *People's Daily*, continues to accord prominence to coverage of Jiang in the papers. Clearly, Jiang does not intend to take a backseat anytime soon.

Not surprisingly, Hu has stated that he will continue with Jiang's policies. Hu also said that his main focus is to concentrate fully on economic construction (聚精会神搞建设，一心一意谋发展).[10] Indeed, Hu is unlikely to introduce any radical or controversial policies that would complicate or even undermine his efforts at consolidating power.

---

[7] Deng mapped out a three-stage growth strategy in 1979 as part of his plan to kick-start China's moribund economy. The first step envisaged by Deng was the doubling of the 1980 GDP by the year 1990. The goal then was to achieve a state of *wenbao* or a state where the people were well-fed and clothed. The second step envisaged by Deng was a doubling of the 1990 GDP by 2000. The goal was to achieve a well-off state or *xiaokang*. Deng's third step was to achieve full-scale modernisation by 2050 although he did not spell out any targets.

[8] *People's Daily*, November 9, 2002.

[9] *International Herald Tribune*, November 21, 2002.

[10] *Ming Pao*, November 28, 2002; *Ming Pao*, November 30, 2002.

Yet, to a great degree, Hu is in a better position than Jiang when the latter was thrust into the limelight in 1989. Unlike Jiang, Hu has successfully weathered a 10-year apprenticeship at the pinnacle of power. This is no mean achievement and is testimony to Hu's intelligence, political astuteness and tenacity in the face of adversity. He can also tap on his network of supporters in the Communist Youth League, Qinghua University and Central Party School, but he should do so without unduly alarming the other Politburo Standing Committee members whose support he needs.

In the initial years at least, Hu will have a tough time being his own man given the predominance of Jiang's faction. In addition, there is Jiang's likely continued involvement in some key decision-making areas such as military affairs and foreign relations, especially the Taiwan affairs. Not only has Hu not secured Jiang's unequivocal support but he is hemmed in by Jiang's supporters in key Party and government organisation. It is too early to speculate if Hu would be a one-term Party Secretary; what is certain is that he would have to live under Jiang's shadow for some time.

Appendix
The Political Bureau and Its Standing Committee at the 15th Party Congress (1997)

	Name	Age	Education
Members of Standing Committee Average age: 65.4	Jiang Zemin	71	Jiaotong Univ. & Soviet Union
	Li Peng	69	Soviet Union
	Zhu Rongji	69	Qinghua Univ.
	Hu Jintao	55	Qinghua Univ.
	Li Ruihuan	63	Beijing Architecture Institute
	Wei Jianxing*	66	Dalian Engrg. Institute
	Li Lanqing*	65	Fudan Univ. & Soviet Union
Members of Political Bureau (excluding Standing Committee) Average age: 61.9	Ding Guan'gen	68	Jiaotong Univ.
	Tian Jiyun	68	Middle School
	Li Changchun*	53	Ha'erbin Industrial Univ.
	Li Tieying	61	Czechoslovakia
	Wu Bangguo	56	Qinghua Univ.
	Wu Guanzheng*	59	Qinghua Univ.
	Chi Haotian*	68	PLA Military School
	Zhang Wannian*	69	PLA Nanjing Military School
	Luo Gan*	62	Beijing Steel Institute
	Jiang Chunyun	67	Chinese Language Univ.
	Jia Qinglin*	57	Hebei Engrg. Institute
	Qian Qichen	69	Junior College & Soviet Union
	Huang Ju	59	Qinghua Univ.
	Wen Jiabao*	55	Beijing Geology Institute
	Xie Fei	65	Middle School
	Zeng Qinghong	58	Beijing Engrg. Institute
	Wu Yi	59	Beijing Petroleum Institute

* Newly recruited members

CHINA'S POLITICS IN 2002 AND PROSPECTIVE CHANGES IN 2003

ZHENG Yongnian & LYE Liang Fook

EXECUTIVE SUMMARY

1. The 16th Party Congress that dominated China's political landscape in 2002 ushered in the first ever smooth and peaceful leadership transition in the history of the Chinese Communist Party (CCP). A fresh and younger team has taken over the helm.
2. Although leadership transition has almost concluded, power succession has only just begun. Jiang Zemin remains influential. It is still unclear whether the triumvirate comprising Hu Jintao, Zeng Qinghong and Wen Jiabao can work together as a team.
3. While the Congress has allocated key positions in the Party, the line-up of government personnel will only be unveiled at the 10th National People's Congress in March 2003. Jiang appears determined to staff more of his men in the next State Council.
4. In preparing for the Congress, the Party propaganda machinery went into overdrive extolling the achievements of Jiang and the Party. Besides tightening Party discipline, the authorities exerted greater control over the print and electronics media.
5. Aside from personnel arrangements, meticulous preparation went into the drafting of Jiang's political report to the Congress that encompassed the "Three Represents" theory. Jiang closely supervised the work of the drafting committee even though Hu Jintao was its chairman.
6. In economic terms, Jiang's vision to transform China into a *xiaokang shehui* (comfortable society) is a long-term strategy to redistribute wealth through growth and to step up economic development in the backward hinterland. In ideological terms,

xiaokang shehui is an affirmation of China's determination to chart its own political development path.
7. In the midst of consolidating power, the 4th generation leadership will have to grapple with a number of pressing issues such as worsening unemployment and corruption, as well as meeting the aspirations of the people for greater accountability and transparency in the Party and government.
8. If Hu is able to bridge the interests of the disparate factions within the Party and government to tackle these challenges, he would enhance his stature and buttress the legitimacy of the leadership. Jiang will then be left with less reason to remain on the political stage.

CHINA'S POLITICS IN 2002 AND PROSPECTIVE CHANGES IN 2003

ZHENG Yongnian & LYE Liang Fook

Ensuing Power Succession

The 16th Party Congress was the singular event that dominated China's political landscape in 2002. Virtually all work on the political front for the entire year was related to or geared towards this major event.

The political manoeuverings intensified as the incumbents jostled with each other to secure the best possible outcomes for themselves and their supporters. Prior to the Congress, the possible line-up of the 4th generation leadership, their political affiliations and policy inclinations became focal points of discussion by China watchers. Speculation was rife on who would occupy key positions in the Party.

The Congress not only ushered in the first ever smooth and peaceful leadership transition in the Party's history but is also noteworthy in terms of the scale of change. A fresh and younger team under Hu Jintao's leadership has been appointed to the

Politburo and its Standing Committee. The old guards, with the exception of Jiang Zemin, have agreed to relinquish their senior party positions and left the affairs of the Party and state to the 4th generation leadership.

While leadership transition has almost concluded, power succession has only just begun. Although Hu Jintao is the highest office bearer in the Party, it is unclear who calls the shots. Jiang has yet to fully retire from the political stage in his capacity as Chairman of the Central Military Commission. He is still ranked No. 1, ahead of Hu, in terms of protocol.

The Chinese military, for one, continues to pledge allegiance to Jiang. In the December issue of the Party's magazine, *Qiushi* (求是), Lieutenant General Zhu Qi, a PLA officer in charge of the security of Beijing, said that the retention of Jiang in the top military post was "an important political choice made by the Party".[1] Jiang is likely to retain this position beyond the 10th National People's Congress (NPC) in March 2003.

Uncertainty also prevails over the kind of working relationship that will unfold among the triumvirate Hu Jintao, Zeng Qinghong and Wen Jiabao. In particular, it is unknown to what extent Zeng will be willing to defer to Hu in the long haul despite his recent public profession of support for Hu.[2] Furthermore, it is an open question how closely-knit Jiang's faction will be in view of the disparate personalities and interest within this group.

Setting the Right Tone

The Party and government placed particular emphasis on setting the right tone for the Congress. Maintaining nationwide stability and

---

[1] *Qiushi* (求是), December 1, 2002.
[2] *Far Eastern Economic Review*, December 26, 2002.

ensuring minimal disruption to preparations for the Congress assumed urgency in light of a spate of workers' unrest in various parts of China including Heilongjiang, Liaoning, Jilin, Gansu, Guizhou and even Beijing. Instead of new major initiatives, the Party and government concentrated on fine-tuning existing policies, such as sustaining high economic growth, or focusing on issues of concern to the people, such as tackling unemployment and reducing the burden on farmers.

The Party's propaganda machinery went into overdrive extolling the achievements of the Party since the last Congress and in particular Jiang's contributions. A book entitled "Jiang Zemin on Socialism with Chinese Characteristics" containing important reports, speeches, articles, letters and written instructions by Jiang over a thirteen-year period was published. Jiang's pictures appeared alongside Mao Zedong and Deng Xiaoping in public. The *People's Daily* highlighted the overwhelming nationwide support for the Congress. Also, the successful damming of the Three Gorges Dam was deliberately timed a day before the start of the Congress to drum up the celebrative mood.[3]

Party discipline was tightened. Wu Bangguo exhorted cadres not to start or spread political rumours or say anything to tarnish the image of the Party or country. He further called on cadres not to publicly contradict the policies or strategies decided by the Party but to channel their opinions internally.[4] Luo Gan separately called on the Party and the government to be vigilant against disruptive elements such as terrorism, ethnic separatism, religious extremism, internal and external threats, and the Falungong movement.[5]

---

[3] *People's Daily* (人民日报), November 7, 2002.
[4] *Qiushi* (求是), April 16, 2002.
[5] *Ming Pao* (明报), April 10, 2002.

A tighter reign was simultaneously exerted by the Party and the government on the print and electronics media. In June, the Party's Central Propaganda Department issued a directive listing 32 areas where the media should either exercise extreme caution when reporting (e.g. impact of WTO entry on various economic sectors in China) or refrain from doing (e.g. sensationalization of news).[6] In an unprecedented move, eight government bodies[7] came together to launch a nationwide campaign to curb the spread of undesirable information on the domestic Internet network which could affect national security and social stability.[8]

The stress on ensuring a conducive environment for the Congress was not confined to the domestic arena. On foreign policy, the authorities continued to raise China's international profile and build relations with other countries while downplaying disputes. Most significantly, great efforts were made to stabilize China-US relations through high level exchanges of visits and the resumption of bilateral military ties.[9] China's relations with Taiwan was also put on a low key. China did not over-react when Chen Shui-bian described Taiwan's relations with China as "one country on each side" of the

---

[6] *Ming Pao* (明报), June 21, 2002.

[7] The eight government bodies were the Ministry of Public Security, Ministry of Education, Ministry of State Security, Ministry of Information Industry, Ministry of Culture, State Administration for Industry and Commerce, State Council Information Office and State Bureau of Secrecy.

[8] *Ming Pao* (明报), May 3, 2002. An attempt was also made to block access by locals to log on to the internationally renowned search engine *Google* but to no avail. It is widely believed that this move was prompted by *Google's* ability to lead Chinese users to sites considered undesirable by the authorities.

[9] In his address to Qinghua University students during his visit to China in February 2002, Bush welcomed the emergence of a "strong, peaceful and prosperous China", a much more conciliatory tone compared to the start of his administration. Hu Jintao was virtually accorded Head of State treatment when he visited the US in April. Jiang also met Bush at his Texas ranch in October, an invitation extended only to close friends of the US President.

Taiwan Straits. China further consolidated relations with its southern neighbours by signing a framework agreement with ASEAN to establish a China-ASEAN Free Trade Zone by 2010.

Key Personnel Arrangements

The jostling for power among the top leadership intensified. While Zhu Rongji had indicated early that he would be relinquishing his senior party post at the Congress and giving up his premiership in March 2003, neither Jiang nor Li Ruihuan ever stated their intention in such unequivocal terms. Li Ruihuan at 68 was below the mandatory retirement age limit of 70 for Politburo members and technically, could still remain on the Politburo Standing Committee. It was expected that Li Ruihuan would be the most senior and experienced member in the Politburo Standing Committee whom Hu Jintao would have to work closely with should Jiang, Li Peng and Zhu Rongji step down.

As for Jiang, speculation was rife that he would either fully retire or surrender only his Party and government positions while retaining the top military post. Up till the eve of the Congress it was not altogether clear what the final outcome would be. Jiang kept his future plans close to his chest and used it as a bargaining chip to secure positions of influence for himself and his supporters. Incessant calls by Jiang's supporters urging him to stay on or exhorting others to rally under his leadership added to the uncertainty. In a speech at the Guangdong Party School in July, Li Changchun, Party Secretary, urged Guangdong party cadres at all levels to keep in line with the leadership, with Jiang at the core.[10]

---

[10] *South China Morning Post*, July 29, 2002.

The PLA, in particular, was one of Jiang's ardent advocates. On separate occasions in January and June, General Fu Quanyou, former Chief of General Staff, called on the Chinese military to obey the core of the Party and military leadership led by Jiang "no matter when and under whatever circumstances".[11] General Chi Haotian, Defence Minister, echoed the same message in June.[12] These statements were strong pledges of allegiance to a person, not to an office. Jiang himself fueled speculation that he would retain his military authority after the Congress when he promoted seven PLA officers to the rank of full general in June.

The Beidaihe meeting in July, where China's top leaders gather for their annual retreat, failed to finalize the leadership line-up for the Congress. The subsequent announcement that the Congress would be held in November, rather than September as earlier speculated, fueled talks of intense wrangling among the top leaders. Opposition to Jiang's staying on came from two main quarters within the Party. First, Li Ruihuan had apparently offered to step down from the Politburo Standing Committee, although not required to do so, to exert pressure on Jiang. Second, discordant notes were sounded by Wei Jianxing, from Qiao Shi's faction, decrying Jiang's unwillingness to relinquish power. Jiang was portrayed as reneging on his pledge to make room for a new generation of leaders when he forced Qiao Shi to retire in 1997.

To counter these challenges, Jiang mounted an ideological offensive by enunciating the "New Three Talks (新三讲)" with its stresses on "Solidarity (讲团结), the Big Picture (讲大局) and Stability (讲稳定)". Although the "New Three Talks" was first mentioned in Jiang's May 31st speech, it gained greater prominence

---

[11] *People's Liberation Army Daily* (解放军报), January 9, 2002 and *People's Liberation Army Daily* (解放军报), June 29, 2002.
[12] *People's Liberation Army Daily* (解放军报), June 25, 2002.

when the *People's Daily* gave front page coverage to an article on this topic.[13] The article appeared to be directed at containing unwarranted rumours originating from Party cadres on personnel arrangements at the highest level as well as the unhealthy jostling for power among them. This was Jiang's message to his political supporters and foes alike to rally to the Party and nation's cause and not do anything to upset the leadership transition as orchestrated by Jiang.

The reshufflings of key positions in Beijing and at the provincial level up till the eve of the Congress gave some indication of who would be among the leadership line-up. Most significantly, the majority of those reshuffled were Jiang's men. In October, Zeng Qinghong relinquished his post as Head of the Party's Organization Department, indicating that he would finally be elevated to the Politburo Standing Committee, a position which eluded him for years. He Guoqiang, Chongqing Party Secretary, replaced Zeng as Head of the Organization Department. Also, Liu Yunshan was appointed Head of the Central Propaganda Department.[14] Around the same time, Jia Qinglin, Beijing Party Secretary, and Huang Ju, Shanghai Party Secretary, were moved to the Party central.[15] All five of them subsequently either became members of the Politburo or its Standing Committee.

Jiang, however, did not completely have his way in deciding the leadership line-up. The expansion of the Politburo Standing Committee from seven to nine showed the compromise that was struck among the various factions in the Party and government. To some extent, the outcome of the leadership line-up is a reflection of

---

[13] *People's Daily* (人民日报), July 22, 2002.

[14] *Xinhua News Agency*, October 24, 2002.

[15] The posts vacated by Jia Qinglin and Huang Ju were filled by Liu Qi and Chen Liangyu respectively, both of whom were politically acceptable to Jiang.

the institutionalization of factional politics, albeit one predominantly in favour of Jiang's faction.

Final Ideological Preparations

Meticulous preparation went into the drafting of Jiang's political report to the Congress. The Politburo Standing Committee decided to form the drafting committee of the political report in October 2001 chaired by Hu Jintao and which included Zeng Qinghong and Wen Jiabao. Teng Wensheng, head of the Party's Policy Research Office and Jiang's ally, was responsible for the actual drafting. The drafting committee was tasked to come up with a report that would guide China to further the goal of building socialism with Chinese characteristics.

In order to come up with a comprehensive report, the drafting committee collated inputs from relevant government departments and Party organizations as well as conducted site visits to various provinces. As early as August 2001, the relevant Party organizations formed fourteen discussion groups to examine issues such as Party building, the overall situation in the country, the development of advanced productive forces and culture, and distribution of income. Hu Jintao chaired meetings to collate the views of these discussion groups. Also, the drafting committee formed eight groups to conduct site visits to 16 locations throughout the country including Guangdong, Jiangsu, Shanghai, Heilongjiang and Gansu. During the site visits, a total of 80 seminars were held involving 914 people.[16]

Even though Hu Jintao was chairman of the drafting committee, Jiang closely supervised its work and intervened to ensure that it was on the right track. In a meeting with the drafting committee in

---

[16] See http://news.xinhuanet.com/newscentre/2002-11/20/content_634795.htm for background to the drafting of the political report to the 16th Party Congress.

January 2002, Jiang set the theme of the political report which is to hold high the banner of Deng Xiaoping Theory, fully imbibe the thinking behind the "Three Represents" theory and construct a full fledged *xiaokang shehui* (全面建设小康社会). Following this meeting, the drafting committee came up with the framework of the report and submitted it first to Jiang and then the Politburo Standing Committee for approval in February. After several revisions, a draft of the report was ready in May which was again submitted to the Politburo Standing Committee for deliberation.

Jiang's May 31st speech at the Central Party School, which traditionally is a platform for important pronouncements, gave the first public indication of the key elements that would be included in the political report.[17] Jiang elaborated on the theme he stated in January. Most significantly, Jiang's speech showed that opposition to his "Three Represents" theory had waned and that there was now more support than when it was first enunciated in February 2000. Jiang's speech also indicated that there was an emerging consensus that the admission of capitalist and private entrepreneurs was necessary for the Party's survival.

Not surprisingly, Hu Jintao was one of the staunchest supporters of Jiang's "Three Represents" theory. In an address at the Central Party School in September, Hu extolled the "Three Represents" theory and called on Party officials to back Jiang's political vision.[18] More significantly, Hu unveiled in July new regulations on the selection and naming of Party and government leaders. According to Hu, these regulations were aimed at evaluating new leaders based on how they imbibed and implemented Jiang's "Three Represents" theory. Cadres who embraced the important ideology of the "Three Represents" were to be promoted.[19]

---

[17] *People's Daily* (人民日报), June 1, 2002.
[18] *South China Morning Post*, September 3, 2002.
[19] *People's Daily* (人民日报), July 23, 2002.

There were, however, dissenting voices from pro-reform liberals and hard-line communists criticizing Jiang's record although they were not serious enough to upset his plans. In a scathing attack on Jiang's "Three Represents" theory, Bao Tong, a former aide to purged party leader Zhao Ziyang and a *de facto* spokesman for liberals in China's political elite, asserted that the Party has abandoned the workers and peasants and become an authoritarian Party representing the rich and powerful. Rather than heralding the onset of democracy with the theory, Bao Tong contends that the Party is on the demise.[20] Aside from Bao Tong, two letters written by conservative critics accused Jiang of abandoning the ideals of the Party by welcoming capitalists into its ranks. The organizer of one of the letters is believed to have ties to Party elder Song Ping, known to be critical of Jiang.[21]

Jiang's name was eventually not included next to the "Three Represents" theory in the Party Constitution, an astute concession by Jiang not to appear over-bearing and as a political trade-off to assign more of his men to key positions in the Party. In any case, Jiang has scored a personal victory and sealed his legacy by having the theory included in the Party Constitution. The theory has entered the pantheon of Chinese revolutionary thought, sharing a status on par with Marxism-Leninism, Mao Zedong Thought and Deng Xiaoping Theory.

Xiaokang Shehui

Jiang's vision to transform the whole of China into a *xiaokang shehui* (comfortable society) is as important as, if not more so than,

---

[20] Bao Tong wrote a 15-page essay which was reviewed by *The Wall Street Journal*. Excerpts of it was reproduced in "China's Unrepresentative Communists", *Asian Wall Street Journal*, August 28, 2002.

[21] *Asian Wall Street Journal*, August 28, 2002.

his "Three Represents" theory although it has received comparatively less attention in the western media. The importance the Party attaches to this vision was underscored by the use of *xiaokang shehui* as the title of Jiang's political report.[22]

The vision to transform the entire country into a *xiaokang shehui* has significant economic implications. It reflects a need to change the pattern of China's economic growth. The emphasis, hitherto, has largely been on unbridled economic growth with wealth concentrated in the coastal provinces and cities while pockets of poverty remain scattered around the country, especially in the inland provinces and rural areas. Jiang's vision aims to address this lopsided development by re-distributing wealth to a larger proportion of the population. This does not imply that China is turning its back on the market economy but rather that increased attention will be placed on re-distributing wealth through growth and stepping up economic development in the backward hinterland. This is a gradual and long-term strategy.

The term *xiaokang shehui* is also politically significant for the following two reasons. First, in ideological terms, it is not only a rejection of the "middle class" concept used in the West but is also by extension a denouncement of the Western notion of liberal democracy. In the West, the development of the middle class is inextricably linked to the onset of democracy. Although detractors may argue that *xiaokang shehui* is nothing but a communist jargon of the middle class, in reality, the significance extends beyond a mere change of term. The Party is telling the whole country and the rest of the world that it intends to chart its own political development path.

---

[22] Jiang has set the target of quadrupling China's GDP by 2020 with 2000 as base year. According to Dr Li Jinwen, one of the drafters of China's 10th Five Year Plan (2001–2005), this would mean achieving a GDP of around US$4 trillion by 2020 with a per capital income of US$3,100. See *The Sunday Times*, November 10, 2002.

It is no coincidence that in the same political report, Jiang rejected China developing along the path of western liberal democracy.

Second, *xiaokang shehui* is not only intellectually appealing to the Chinese people, many of whom still yearn for a better life, but also politically sound because it propounds the attractive notion that everybody could eventually attain at least a comfortable standard of living.

10th National People's Congress

While the Congress has allocated key positions in the Party, the key positions in the government has yet to be officially confirmed although there are indications of who they might go to. The next political milestone in China is the 10th NPC in March 2003 where the line-up of key government personnel will be unveiled. Hu Jintao is expected to assume the Presidency from Jiang in line with past practice where the General Secretary is also the Head of State. However, Hu is unlikely to be the main player in China's relations with other countries as Zeng Qinghong is likely to have a role to play possibly as Vice President.

Wen Jiabao looks set to become Premier in March 2003. What is unclear is to what extent Jiang's men will occupy positions in the next State Council.[23] There are indications that Jiang is determined to staff more of his men in key positions in this institution. In December, Zhou Yongkang was appointed to head the Ministry of Public Security, the first time a Politburo member was made public security minister since the end of the Cultural Revolution.[24] Zhou's

---

[23] Traditionally, Jiang's influence has extended to the Party, military and foreign policy and he has largely refrained from interfering too much in the affairs of the State Council.

[24] *South China Morning Post*, December 11, 2002.

appointment suggests that law and order has assumed new significance in the eyes of the leadership. Interestingly, Zhou has also been made Vice Chief of the Central Commission of Politics and Law headed by Luo Gan, Li Peng's protégé.

Zeng Peiyan, Minister of State Development Planning Commission, is tipped to become Secretary General of the State Council or possibly even Vice Premier. Zeng has vast economic experience as China's top economic planner and has been one of a handful of top officials to address the NPC at its annual session on the state of the Chinese economy. Another possible candidate for Vice Premier is Huang Ju who has been credited with Shanghai's remarkable economic progress. As for Wu Bangguo, he is expected to relinquish his post as Vice Premier and move to head the NPC. Jia Qinglin is slated to become Chairman of the Chinese People's Political Consultative Committee, a post previously held by Li Ruihuan who used it to build up an independent power base.

If Jiang's men were to occupy more positions in the government, especially in the State Council, it would affect Wen Jiabao's ability to run the affairs of the state. However, there is a limit to how many men Jiang can appoint as they would need to have the necessary expertise to operate effectively wherever they are assigned to and earn the respect of their subordinates. The State Council has over the years become much less ideological and more technocratic in its orientation as the complexities of the challenges confronting the country require ever more specific and comprehensive solutions to address them.[25] Wen Jiabao is expected to deepen this trend.

---

[25] Zhu Rongji has in no small measure contributed to this trend with his streamlining of government bureaucracy and reforms in key economic sectors such as taxation, finance and banking.

Challenges to 4th Generation Leadership

In the midst of consolidating power, the 4th generation leadership under Hu Jintao is unlikely to come up with any new major policy initiatives. Instead, the leadership would have to come up to speed to grapple with a number of pressing issues. How these issues are handled will to a large extent reflect Hu's ability to bridge the interests of disparate factions within the Party and government to work together as a team. If he is successful in this endeavour, Hu would enhance his stature and buttress the legitimacy of the leadership to govern on its own merit. This would invariably hasten Jiang's full retirement from the political stage.

Hu's overriding priority is to ensure that stability continues to prevail in the country. In one of his early moves since taking over as General Secretary, Hu convened a meeting of the Central Leading Group on National Security in late November where he assumed the chairmanship of the group from Jiang.[26] This will not only help Hu to consolidate power but is also an indication of the paramount importance the leadership attaches to stability. The group, comprising senior civilian and military personnel including Zeng Qinghong, Wen Jiabao, Guo Boxiong (Vice Chairman, Central Military Commission), Zhou Yongkang (Minister, Public Security), Xu Yongyue (Minister, National Security), is responsible for preventing any potential threats that could de-stabilize the country.

A significant challenge the leadership faces is to curb the increased incidence of social unrest in the country caused in part by rising levels of unemployment. Officially, China's registered unemployment rate is about 4% but this figure excludes those laid-off (*xiagang*) from state enterprises or the excess labour in the countryside. Jiang himself has highlighted the urgency to find work

---

[26] Among the most important leading groups are those overseeing national security, foreign affairs, finance and economics, and Taiwan affairs.

for a growing army of unemployed.²⁷ The unemployment situation will worsen as China's industries restructure themselves to meet the WTO challenge. Sustaining high economic growth in order to generate sufficient jobs will be the leadership's top priority.

Another significant challenge confronting the leadership is the continuing scourge of corruption and misconduct by cadres and government officials that has tarnished the Party and government image and eroded their legitimacy. If left unchecked, the Party could even lose its monopoly on power. Efforts by the authorities to clean up its ranks have been piecemeal at best with actions intended to serve a political purpose. News that 124,000 Party members had been dismissed as a result of disciplinary problems from 1997–2001 was widely perceived as an attempt to shore up the Party's image ahead of the Congress.²⁸ The admission of capitalist and private entrepreneurs into the Party will open up more opportunities for abuse of power, and corruption is expected to become even more rampant.

An additional challenge, one which the present leadership's predecessors have failed to tackle head-on, is political reform. Political reform in China refers to efforts aimed at rendering the workings of the Party and the government more transparent, accountable and "democratic". The key lies in meeting the aspirations of a much more stratified Chinese society while maintaining the Party's grip on power. China has initiated modest steps at political reform with elections introduced fundamentally at the village level in the 1980s. More significantly, the Party now seeks to represent the interests of the entire Chinese people and not that of a particular class. But what kind of political entity the Party will evolve into and whether this transformation will be successful remains to be seen.

---

²⁷ *People's Daily* (人民日报), September 13, 2002.
²⁸ *People's Daily* (人民日报), September 2, 2002. The sacking of Wang Xuebing, former President of China Construction Bank, from the Party on corruption charges was also seen in the same light.

Appendix
Major Political Events in 2002

Feb 21–22	President George Bush visits China.
Mar 4	Large-scale demonstration by tens of thousands of disgruntled workers dismissed by Daqing Oil Management Bureau in Heilongjiang. Also, in Liaoyang, thousands of factory workers take to the streets on March 11 over unpaid wages and alleged embezzlement by employers. On March 27, over 200 workers at a car factory in Beijing protest over failure to receive retirement benefits.
Mar 4–18	5th Session of the 9th National People's Congress.
Mar 9	According to a Pentagon classified report, the Bush Administration has instructed its military to review its nuclear policy including envisaging the use of nuclear weapons against China in the event of war across the Taiwan Straits.
Mar 10–12	Taiwan's Defence Minister Tang Yao-ming visits Florida to attend the US-Taiwan Defence Summit 2002 organized by the US-Taiwan Business Council. He is Taiwan's first Defence Minister to be granted an entry visa to enter the US since Washington switched recognition from Taipei to Beijing in 1979.
Mar 25	China successfully launches an unmanned spacecraft, Shenzhen III, from the Jiuquan launch centre in northern Gansu. China aims to put a man in space by 2005.

Apr 2–10	Li Peng visits Japan to commemorate the 30th Anniversary of the establishment of diplomatic relations between the two countries.
Apr 24	About 300–400 workers protest in Lanzhou against job losses in the oil industry, apparently emboldened by the protests that occurred in Daqing and Liaoyang.
Apr 27–May 3	Hu Jintao goes on his first ever visit to the US in his capacity as Vice President. Before that, Hu visited Malaysia and Singapore from Apr 24–26.
May 1	Workers in Heilongjiang, Liaoning and Guizhou stage demonstrations demanding greater government attention to the plight of unemployed and laid-off workers.
Jun 2	Jiang Zemin promotes seven senior PLA officers to the rank of full general.
Jun 3–18	Jiang Zemin attends the summit meetings of the Conference on Interaction and Confidence Building Measures in Asia in Kazakhstan and the Shanghai Cooperation Organisation (SCO) in St. Petersburg. Jiang also visits Latvia, Estonia, Iceland and Lithuania.
Late Jul–mid Aug	Chinese leaders' annual retreat at Beidaihe.
Aug 3	Chen Shui-bian describes Taiwan's relations with China as "one country on each side" of the Taiwan Straits.
Aug 25–Sep 6	Zhu Rongji visits Algeria, Morocco, Cameroon and South Africa and attends the World Summit on Sustainable Development in South Africa.

Sep 3–22	Li Peng visits Thailand, Indonesia, the Philippines and Australia.
Sep 19–28	Zhu Rongji attends the 4th ASEM Summit and 5th EU-China Summit held in Denmark and also visits Austria, Denmark and France.
Oct 22–25	Jiang Zemin visits the US, covering Chicago, Houston and Crawford, and meets Bush at his Texas Ranch.
Oct 26–27	Jiang Zemin attends the 10th APEC Leaders' Meeting in Los Cabos, Mexico.
Nov 1–4	Zhu Rongji attends the 6th ASEAN + China, Japan and ROK (10+3) Summit, ASEAN + China (10+1) Summit and Greater Mekong Sub-region Economic Cooperation (GMS) Summit in Phnom Penh, Cambodia.
Nov 3–5	7th Plenum of the 15th Party Congress.
Nov 7	Preparatory Meeting of the 16th Party Congress.
Nov 8–14	16th Party Congress.
Nov 15	1st Plenum of the 16th Party Congress.

CHINA'S ECONOMY IN 2002 AND OUTLOOK FOR 2003

John WONG

EXECUTIVE SUMMARY

1. China's economy in 2002 grew at 8%, up from the 7.3% of 2001. Such growth performance is highly impressive amidst a global economic slowdown.
2. The uptrend started in the second quarter, fuelled by a boom in exports and foreign direct investment. Foreign trade soared by 22% to a record level of US$620 billion. FDI continued to surge to US$53 billion.
3. China has been able to buck the global declining trends in trade and investment partly because much of the world remains economically depressed while China continues to offer a stable and thriving business environment.
4. Excellent external sector performance notwithstanding, China's economic growth in 2002 as in the past was basically underpinned by increases in domestic demand (domestic consumption and investment).
5. As household consumption remained sluggish due to deflationary pressures, the government had to prop up growth with a pro-active fiscal policy by sharply increasing its public sector capital spending. Much of the 2002 growth was in effect the product of a hefty 16.1% rise in fixed asset investment.
6. Prospects for 2003 remain cautiously optimistic, with growth projected to be 7.6–7.8%. The government has declared its readiness to prime pump growth again should external demand falls short. This underscores China's remarkable economic resilience.

7. China has just had a smooth transfer of leadership to the younger fourth generation headed by Hu Jintao. Regardless of how power politics is played out among the young leaders, there would be no sharp alteration in the direction of economic reform and development.
8. This is because China's top leaders across the generations have already reached a broad consensus on all major economic policy directions. Zhu Rongj's economic legacies are also likely to continue, in part because his "right-hand man" Wen Jiabao (slated to succeed Zhu as Premier) has already been heavily involved in all major economic policy decisions for many years.
9. The new leaders, however, will have to address a number of salient economic and social issues. They include rising urban unemployment, growing rural unrest (the "peasant problem") and a large debt burden of the state banks. Sustained economic growth and continuing economic reform are still the best means of coping with these problems.
10. At the 16th Party Congress, Jiang Zemin put forward a radical idea of developing China into a *xiaokang shehui* (a moderately affluent society) by 2020. To achieve this, China needs not only high economic growth but also new strategies that will speed up the distribution of growth benefits more extensively.

CHINA'S ECONOMY IN 2002 AND OUTLOOK FOR 2003

John WONG

Growth Performance beyond Expectations

China's economy in 2002 turned in 8% growth, up from the 7.3% of 2001.[1] For the first time, China's total GDP (gross domestic product) breached the 10 trillion yuan (US$1.2 trillion) mark. Such robust growth is highly impressive against the backdrop of a global economic slowdown. For several years in a row, China has become the best-performing economy in the Asia-Pacific region, if not in the world. (Charts 1 & 2).

China's strong growth in 2002 was widely anticipated in recent months, especially after it registered an average of 7.9% growth for its first three quarters. As shown in Chart 3, the uptrend started in the second quarter and then continued to pick up. This must come as a surprise to China's policy makers who at the beginning of 2002 were

---

[1] "GDP set for 8% growth", *China Daily,* December 31, 2002.

CHART 1 CHINA'S ECONOMIC GROWTH, 1978–2002

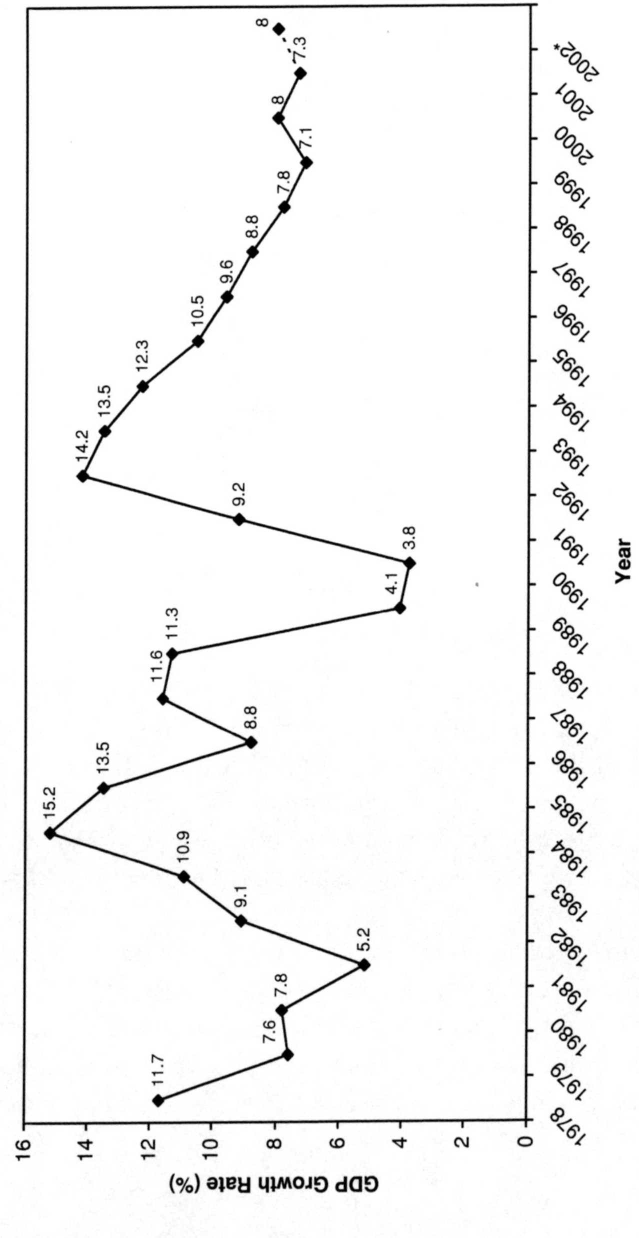

Sources: *China Statistical Yearbook*, various issues.
2002 GDP growth forecast — official sources.

John Wong 51

CHART 2 ECONOMIC PERFORMANCE OF CHINA AND SELECTED ASIAN ECONOMIES, 1996–2002

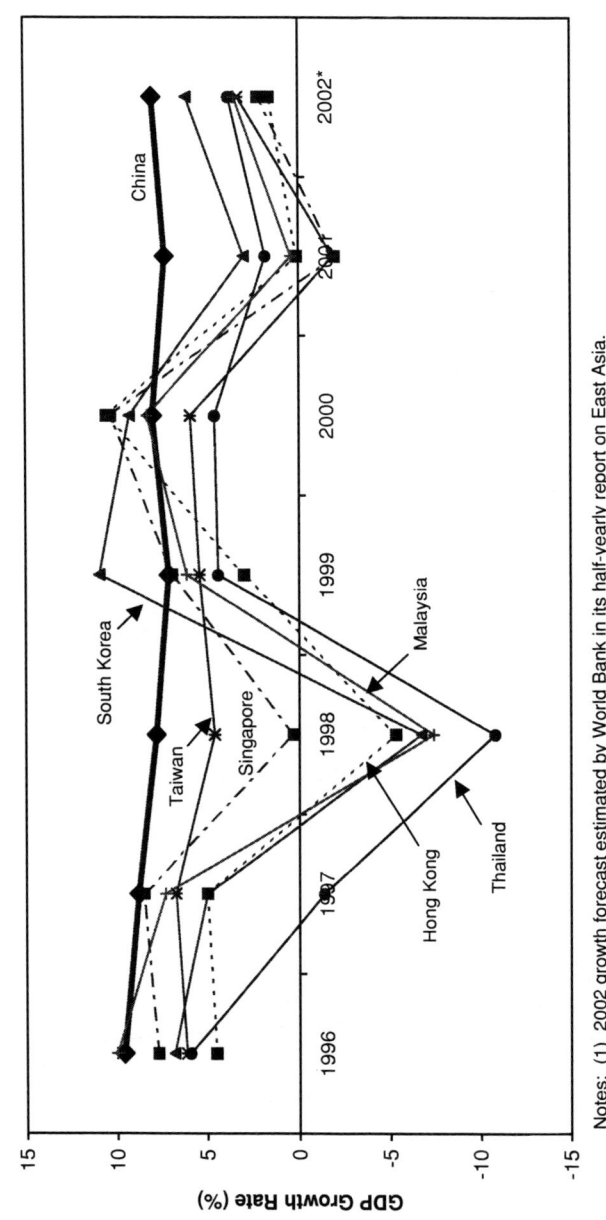

Notes: (1) 2002 growth forecast estimated by World Bank in its half-yearly report on East Asia.
(2) Singapore's official growth rate for 2002 is 2.2%.

Sources: World Bank, "East Asia Regional Update: Making Progress in Uncertain Times", 6 November 2002; *Asian Development Outlook 2002*.

CHART 3 CHINA'S QUARTERLY GROWTH RATE, 1998–2002

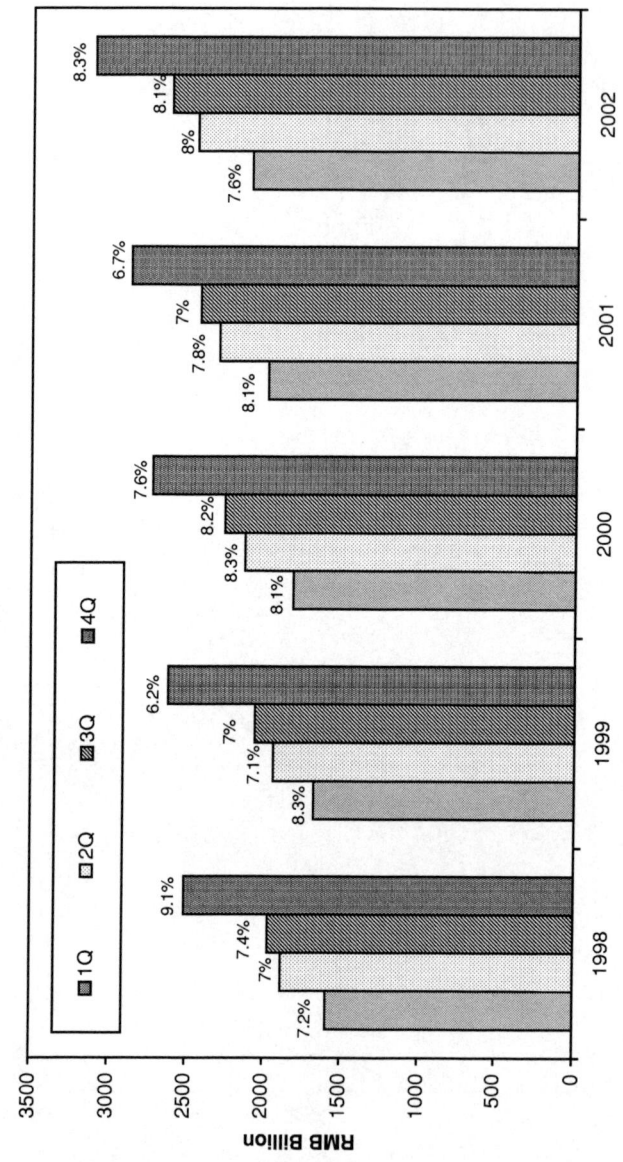

Note: The level of quarter GDP is in current price and the quarter growth rate is calculated in constant price. Estimate for the 4th quarter growth in 2002 is based on the officially estimated 8% GDP growth rate.
Sources: The People's Bank of China, *Quarterly Statistical Bulletin*, various issues; *China Monthly Economic Indicators*, Oct 2002 issue.

expecting only 7% growth on account of the cloudy international economic outlook and China's uncertain adjustment to its first-year WTO membership.

Contrary to the initial forecast at the start of 2002, the external sector performance of the Chinese economy was unexpectedly strong, particularly in the second half. Foreign trade growth, instead of slowing down because of the expected sluggish demand of the developed country markets, had in fact soared by 22% to reach a record OF US$620 billion for the whole year. The influx of foreign direct investment (FDI), after its big rise in 2001 to US$48 billion as foreign businesses rushed to set up beachheads in China in anticipation of its WTO membership, had surged in 2002 to US$53 billion.

China has been able to buck the global declining trends in trade and investment partly because much of the world remains economically depressed while China continues to offer a stable business environment with thriving opportunities.[2] Rising exports and rising FDI are taken by Beijing as clear evidence of China's growing economic competitiveness. They have certainly made it easier for China to cope with the many WTO-related problems, not to mention allaying the early fears of the potentially disruptive WTO effects on its domestic economy. In many ways, China has passed the test of its first-year WTO membership quite smoothly. Both the US and Japanese authorities have given Beijing the credit for having implemented a host of new regulations and new legislations to honour its WTO commitments.

Apart from its excellent external sector performance, China's economic growth in 2002 as in the past, remained basically domestic-demand driven, i.e., its growth stemmed largely from increases in domestic consumption and domestic investment, with

---

[2] "China bucks waning FDI trend", *Asia Times*, October 26, 2002.

external demand (i.e., exports) still playing a statistically small though not an insignificant part. As China in recent years was also affected by the global deflationary trends with falling household consumption, the government had to boost growth by increasing domestic investment. Such is the pro-active fiscal policy, which has been in operation since 1998. In effect, a substantial portion of the 2002 growth was the product of such fiscal stimulus through a sharp rise in fixed asset investment.

At the recent annual high-level economic work conference, chaired by China's newly elected Party leader Hu Jintao, it was decided that the government would continue with its pro-active fiscal policy in order to maintain the existing growth momentum. Economic growth for 2003 was recently forecast to be 7.6–7.8%.[3] China in any case needs a minimum 7% growth to help cope with its myriads of economic and social problems. If external economic conditions were not conducive to growth, the government would prop it up by expanding domestic demand. The fact that China has been able to continue to prime pump growth, almost totally oblivious to the adverse global economic environment, is a mark of its growing economic resilience, something unique only to a large and diverse economy like China.[4]

---

[3] "GDP growth of 7–8% forecast", *China Daily*, December 28, 2002.

[4] There are of course limits to China's pro-active fiscal policy. The central government fiscal deficit, which was only 0.7% of GDP in 1997, rose to about 3% in 2001, the safety limit of EU under the Maastricht Treaty. Because of this, Zhu Rongji was nicknamed "Deficit Premier", much to his chagrin. In China's case, the government can still play around with deficit financing for a few more years because of China's high domestic savings. In the long run, China still has to face the growing national debt if the pro-active fiscal policy was to continue year after year. For more detailed discussion of this subject, see Cui Zhiyuan, "How Serious is China's Fiscal Deficit? Applying EU's 'Golden Rule'", *EAI Background Brief no. 127,* July 16, 2002. China's economists are nowadays openly debating the pros and cons of the pro-active fiscal policy.

Sources of Growth

The pattern of China's economic growth is now pretty much similar to other market economies. As a large, continental sized economy, China's domestic demand (i.e., domestic consumption and domestic investment) regularly accounts for more than 80% of its total demand, thereby constituting the major source of growth. According to our recent study, on average, every 1% increase in domestic consumption in China generates 0.66% more GDP; every 1% increase in domestic investment generates 0.33% more; but every 1% increase in net exports (i.e., exports minus imports) generates only 0.02% more.[5]

China's economy during 1993–1995, as shown in Chart 4, experienced double-digit rates of growth, as Deng Xiaoping's *nanxun* (tour of South China) in 1992 sparked off an explosion of domestic investment, which increased 50–60% a year. As a result, the economy became seriously overheated. It took Premier Zhu Rongji great efforts to cool down the economy by squeezing hard on fixed investment, and so eventually bringing the economy to a soft landing in 1996. After the mid-1990s, China's economy has become less investment driven while household consumption is getting more important. In 1999 the economic growth hit a low of 7.1% as fixed investment growth plunged to 10% and as domestic demand suffered from sluggish growth. After the 1997 Asian financial crisis, fixed investment was manipulated again by Zhu, this time round as an instrument of his expansionary fiscal policy to stimulate growth as domestic deflation set in.

---

[5] For details, see John Wong & Sarah Chan, "Why China's Economy can Sustain High Performance: An Analysis of its Sources of Growth", *EAI Background Brief No. 138,* November 14, 2002.

CHART 4   CHINA'S DOMESTIC INVESTMENT AND DOMESTIC CONSUMPTION GROWTH, 1980–2002

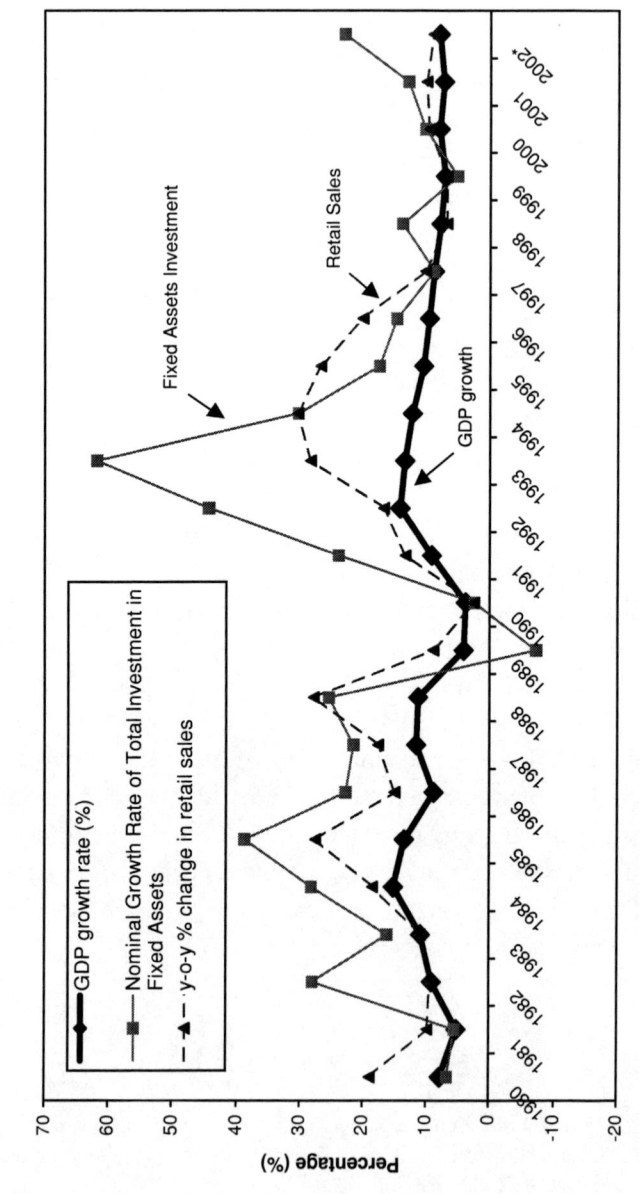

Note: * denotes official estimates for the whole year.
Source: *China Statistical Abstract*, 2002.

What about the sources of growth for 2002? For domestic consumption, total retail sales for the first 11 months of 2002 increased only 8.8%, down by 1.3 percentage points from 2001. This means that China was still experiencing strong deflationary pressures. Indeed, as shown in Chart 5, RPI (retail price index) for the first 11 months of 2002 dropped by 0.8%. China is currently in the midst of a new consumer revolution for its urban population. Urban households are now more or less saturated with the commonly affordable consumer durables. In 2001, every urban household owned on average 1.21 colour TV, 0.82 fridge, 0.92 washing machine, 0.4 camera, and 0.13 personal computer.[6] Though the annual private car sales reached the one million mark for the first time in 2002, this big-ticket item, like private housing, is still beyond the reach of ordinary consumers, who now have to pay much more for services like medical care and education, which are no longer heavily subsidized. All this, including the continuing price deflation, has rendered consumer sentiment generally low.

In the circumstances, the government had to make up for the shortfall in domestic consumption by increasing fixed investment, which in 2002 increased by a hefty 16.1%, compared to 13% for 2001. To sustain such a huge investment spending (mainly for public sector capital expenditure), the government in early 2002 issued 150 billion yuan (US$18 billion) long-term bonds. Domestic investment was further bolstered by a large influx of foreign direct investment (FDI), which in the first 11 months increased 15% and is expected to reach the record level of US$55 billion for 2002 (Chart 6). According to an UNCTAD estimate, global FDI in 2002 will come down to US$530 billion from US$740 billion in

---

[6] "The remarkable change in the consumption pattern of urban inhabitants", www.xinhuane.com/bewscbter/2002/-12/17.

58 CHINA'S ECONOMY IN 2002 AND OUTLOOK FOR 2003

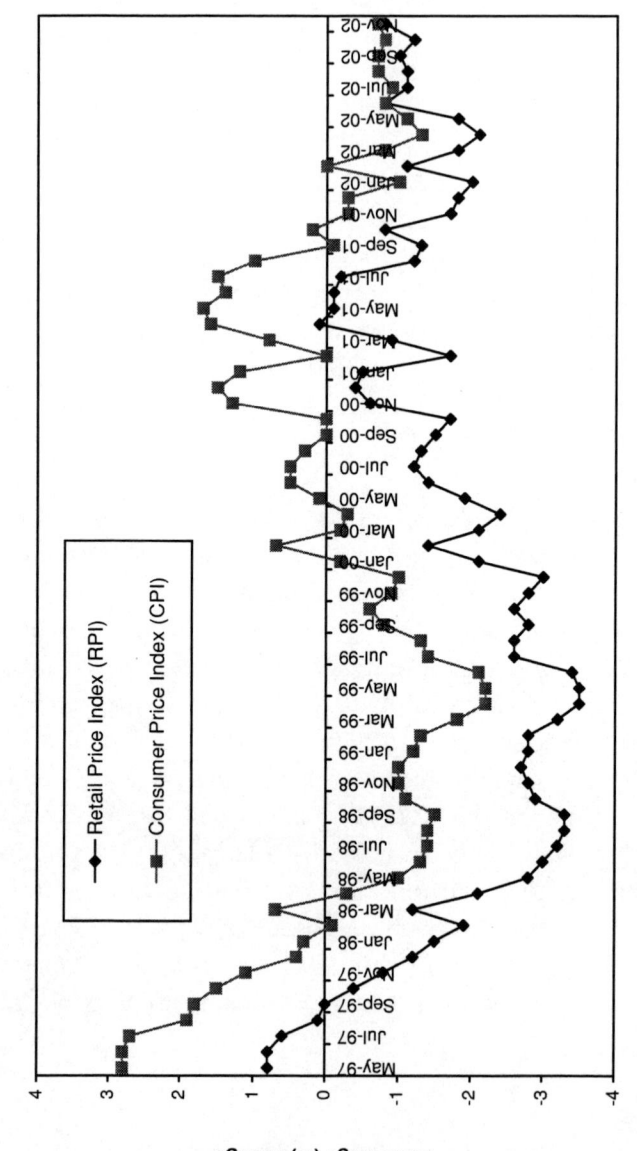

CHART 5 DEFLATIONARY PRESSURES IN CHINA, 1997–2002

Sources: The People's Bank of China, *Quarterly Statistical Bulletin* (various issues); *China Monthly Statistics* (various issues). November monthly data for 2002 data extracted from latest *Xinhua* news reports.

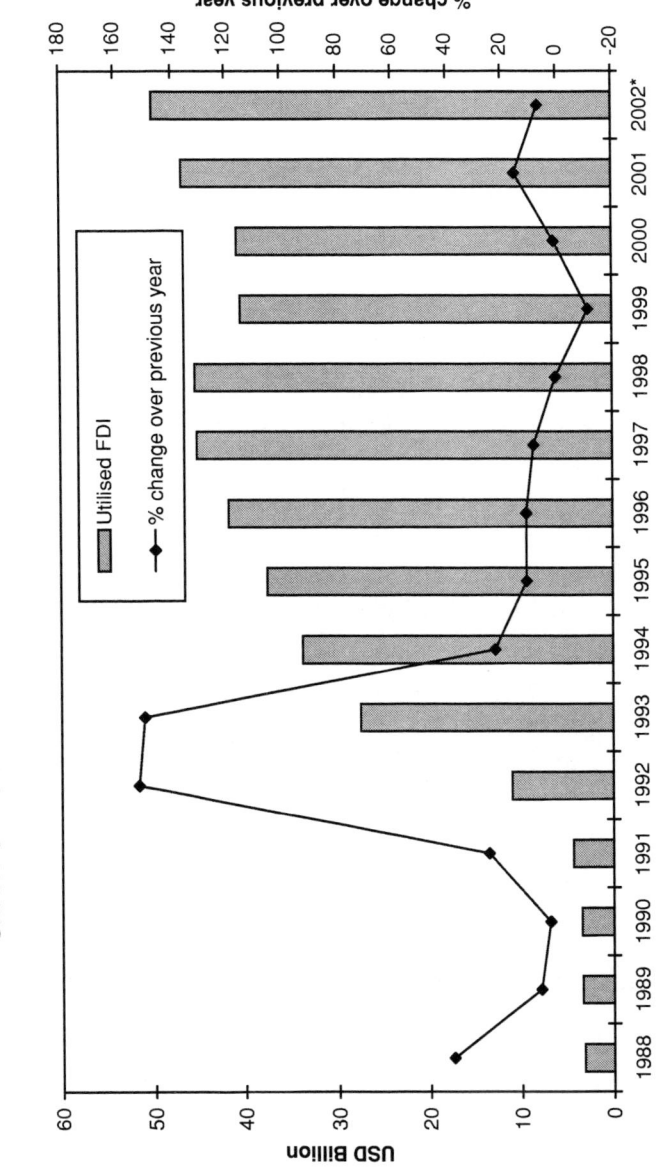

CHART 6   FOREIGN DIRECT INVESTMENT IN CHINA, 1988–2002

Source: *China Statistical Yearbook* (various issues). * FDI for 2002 is officially estimated to reach US$50 billion.

2001, and 10% of it will end up in China, exceeding for the first time the share for the US. In short, China's 2002 economic growth is basically underpinned by the massive domestic investment.

It must be stressed that while domestic demand underpins the "core" growth rate of about 6–7%, it is external demand that provides the extra push for the economy to reach the 8% growth in 2002. Exports for the first 11 months soared by 21.6% to US$294 billion, and China's trade surplus in 2002 is expected to be larger than that of last year (Chart 7). Accordingly, China's total foreign reserves have been steadily building up and are expected by the end of 2002 to reach US$280 billion, the world's second largest after Japan. With such strong external balance, coupled with the gradual decline of the US dollar, the *Renminbi* is under increasing pressures to revalue. But Beijing is likely to resist revaluation for fear of losing its export competitiveness.

As broached earlier, external demand, though nominally accounting for only a small share in China's total demand, is actually making far more significant contribution to the final growth numbers. China's foreign trade sector is the most vibrant segment of the economy. An export boom creates a strong catalyst effect on the rest of the economy by generating extensive multiplier effects on various economic sectors, which are statistically hard to capture. It may be said that just as domestic demand is the prime source of "basic economic growth" for China as a whole, external demand is the engine of its economic boom, particularly for the coastal region.

After Politics, Economic Problems to Surface

2002 was the year of politics for China, with economics taking a backseat, as everything was geared to the 16th Party Congress. This crucial meeting was successfully convened in late November — "successfully" in the sense that it resulted in a wholesale transfer of

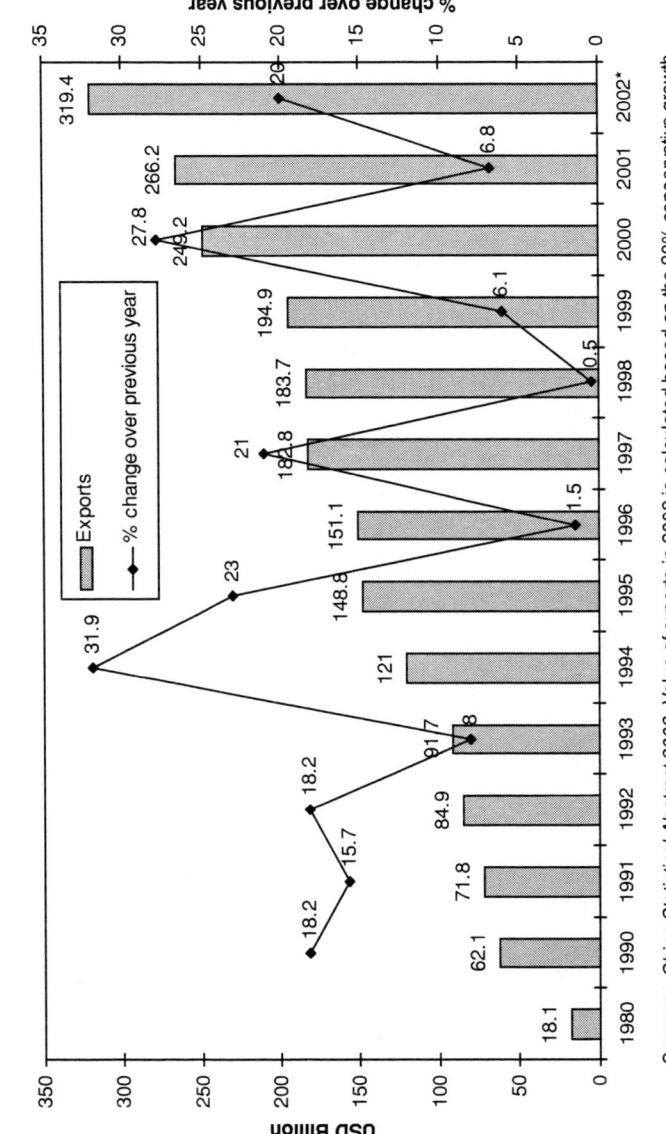

CHART 7 CHINA'S EXPORTS, 1980–2002

Sources: *China Statistical Abstract 2002*. Value of exports in 2002 is calculated based on the 20% conservative growth estimate by Xinhua News Agency, 27 Dec 2002.

leadership positions to the younger fourth generation headed by Hu Jintao. All the old guards, except Jiang Zemin, have openly agreed to step down. Whether or not the present "leadership transition" would result in a real "power transition" to Hu Jintao, there would be no sharp change in the direction of economic policy-making, especially in regard to reform and development.

Fundamentally, China's top leaders across the generations have over the years already reached a broad consensus on all major economic policy directions. Even though Zhu Rongji, dubbed China's "Economic Czar", is soon to give up his premiership, serious disruption in policy making is also unlikely. This is because Zhu's "right-hand man", Wen Jiabao (who is slated to succeed Zhu), has already been heavily involved in all major economic policy decisions for many years. Furthermore, China's State Council is in effect operating much like an "economic cabinet", with most ministers, commissioners and heads of various bureaucracies coming largely from pragmatic and technocratic background. All this augers well for policy continuity. Zhu's main economic legacies are therefore also likely to continue regardless of the outcome of the political jostling among the top political leaders.

By and large, the new economic leadership will (a) domestically, continue with the unfinished business of economic reform, particularly in regard to the state-owned enterprise (SOE) reform and the financial sector reform; (b) externally, continue to expand China's linkages with the global economy within the WTO framework; and (c) continue to minimize the impact on the domestic economy of adverse external economic fluctuations, including any disruptive WTO effects. To better realize these objectives, China's new economic leadership must strive to maintain the existing high growth momentum. Hence the continuation by the new leadership of the past pro-growth policy as the over-arching economic strategy.

At the same time, the new economic leadership cannot be oblivious to several salient economic and social issues that had either cropped up from or been aggravated by past economic growth. They include (a) rising urban unemployment as a result of intensifying the SOE reform; (b) increasing income inequality and regional economic disparity as a result of the government's past relentless and single-minded pursuit of high GDP growth; (c) growing rural unrest as result of the lop-sided, urban-biased development strategy; and (d) a high level of non-performing loans (NPLs) in the state banks, caused in part by the lack of progress in the financial sector reform. These are the burning issues, which are crying out for attention.

Urban unemployment has risen sharply in recent years because of a combination of factors, including SOE reform (which led to *xiagang* or layoffs), WTO-related structural adjustment, and rising new entrants to the labour force. The official unemployment figures, which refer to "registered unemployment", have remained quite low for many years (at around 4%), mainly because they exclude the *xiagang* workers and those who do not have legal residence status (*hukou*). The actual unemployment rate in urban areas is more like 7–8%, which is sufficiently serious. For China, as elsewhere, only sustained economic growth can offer effective long-term solution to the unemployment problem.

The issue of bad-debt in China's state banks has recently received much media attention.[8] Official estimates put current NPLs of the four state banks at 25% of their total loans (down from 29% a year ago). But foreign credit rating agencies put China's NPL ratio at 40 to 50%, a level that is much higher than that for Thailand and South Korea on the eve of the 1997 Asian financial crisis. Nobody really

---

[8] For instance, "China's banking troubles cast a long shadow", *International Herald Tribune,* December 20, 2002; and "Focus on bade-debt burden", *China Daily*, December 5, 2002.

knows the exact NPL levels of Chinese banks due to the lack of transparency and China's different accounting standards.

Suffice to say, China's NPL problem is getting serious, because excessive bad debt hampers the efficient functioning of the banking system.[9] But foreign commentators also tend to exaggerate China's NPL problem. It may be stressed that bank loans in China come mainly from domestic savings deposits, with both lenders and borrowers being state agents and thereby under the firm control of the government. This, together with China's strong external economic balance, makes it most unlikely for a large-scale banking crisis to blow up in China. So long as China can sustain its high economic growth, the bad debt can eventually be digested.

By far the greatest challenge to the new leadership is the "peasant problem" (*nongmin wenti*), which had already haunted the old leadership under Jiang. The peasant problem (which covers three aspects: the peasant, the agricultural sector, and the village, and hence the so-called *san-nong* problems) is, strictly speaking, a problem of development. Industrialization everywhere is accompanied by an inevitable decline of agriculture as its resources and employment continuously shift to the urban sector. In China, the agricultural decline has been badly managed partly because of the explosive industrial growth in the last decade and partly because the existing development strategies have built into themselves many blatantly anti-rural policies. Their high tax burdens apart, rural inhabitants enjoy very few of the state subsidies available to urban inhabitants. As a result, rural-urban income gaps continue to widen. All this adds up to potential rural unrest, which can undermine China's overall economic progress.

---

[9] It was recently reported that Beijing had set up a high-level inter-ministerial "Central Leading Group on Financial Sector Security", whose job is to protect China against falling into a financial crisis.

At the 16th Party Congress, Jiang Zemin put forward a radical idea of developing China into a *xiaokang shehui* (a moderately well-off society) by 2020. *"Xiaokang"* as a socio-economic target of development was first raised by Deng Xiaoping in the early 1980s. Today, the more developed part of China, i.e., the coastal region, has by and large achieved *"xiaokang"* in terms of having satisfied the basic needs of the people, whereas the vast rural hinterland is still badly lagging behind. Jiang now wants development to reach the whole of China (*"xiaokang* in an all-round way"). To achieve this, China will need to continue with its high economic growth and to develop a new redistributive mechanism that can trickle down the growth benefits more rapidly and more extensively. Such is a daunting challenge for the present new leaders as well as their successors.

ABOUT THE AUTHORS

John WONG

Professor John Wong is Research Director of the East Asian Institute at the National University of Singapore. He was formerly Director of the Institute of East Asian Political Economy (1990–1996). His publications include *Land Reform in the People's Republic of China* (1973), *ASEAN Economies in Perspective* (1978) and *Understanding China's Socialist Market Economy* (1994), as well as numerous papers on the economic development of China, ASEAN and Asian NIEs. Recent books which he co-edited include *China's Political Economy* (1998); *Hong Kong in China: Challenges of Transition* (1999); *China: Two Decades of Reform and Change* (1999); *China's Emerging New Economy* (2000); and *China's Economy Into The New Century* (2002).

ZHENG Yongnian

Zheng Yongnian is Senior Research Fellow of the East Asian Institute at the National University of Singapore. He is also a recipient of SSRC-MacArthur Foundation Fellowship and John D. and Catherine T. MacArthur Foundation Fellowship. Zheng's publications have appeared in various journals such as *Political Science Quarterly*, *Asian Survey*, *Pacific Review*, *Japanese Journal of Political Science*, and *Third World Quarterly*. He is the author of *Discovering Chinese Nationalism in China* (1999), and *Globalization and State Transformation in China* (forthcoming). He is co-editor of *Reform, Legitimacy and Dilemma* (2000), *The Nanxun Legacy and China's Post-Deng Development* (2001), and *China's Post-Jiang Leadership Succession* (2002).

LYE Liang Fook

Lye Liang Fook is Research Officer of the East Asian Institute at the National University of Singapore. Having served in Singapore's Ministry of Foreign Affairs previously, he is now pursuing his interest in academia.